HEALTH HEROES

I'M A PARAMEDIC

LAUREN KUKLA

ILLUSTRATED BY SUSANA GURREA

MAYO CLINIC PRESS KIDS

With gratitude to Hanan Wazwaz, Paramedic

MAYO CLINIC PRESS KIDS | An imprint of Mayo Clinic Press
200 First St. SW
Rochester, MN 55905
MCPress.MayoClinic.org

To stay informed about Mayo Clinic Press, please subscribe to our free e-newsletter at MCPress.MayoClinic.org or follow us on social media.

For bulk sales contact Mayo Clinic at SpecialSalesMayoBooks@mayo.edu.

Proceeds from the sale of every book benefit important medical research and education at Mayo Clinic.

ISBN: 9798887701202 (paperback) | 9798887701103 (library binding) | 9798887701547 (ebook) | 9798887701127 (multiuser PDF) | 9798887701110 (multiuser ePub)

Library of Congress Control Number: 2023024378
Library of Congress Cataloging-in-Publication Data is available upon request.

TABLE OF CONTENTS

CHAPTER 1

HELLO!

Hello! My name is Justin Chen. I'm a paramedic! I provide emergency medical care to people who are sick or hurt. I take them safely to the hospital if needed.

I love my job because I get to help people. Every day is different. And no matter what, I do my best to take care of all my patients!

Paramedics often work for hospitals or ambulance companies. Some paramedics work for fire departments. Others work on planes, helicopters, or ships!

I am a paramedic for a hospital. But I spend most of my **shift** in the ambulance.

CHAPTER 2

A PARAMEDIC'S TOOL KIT

Being a paramedic takes special skills. Paramedics need to show patients kindness and respect. We need to be able to think on our feet. But there are also tools that help me do my job.

JUMP BAG

To carry supplies to an emergency **scene**. It holds bandages, scissors, gloves, and many other medical supplies.

MEDICATION BAG

Holds life-saving medications

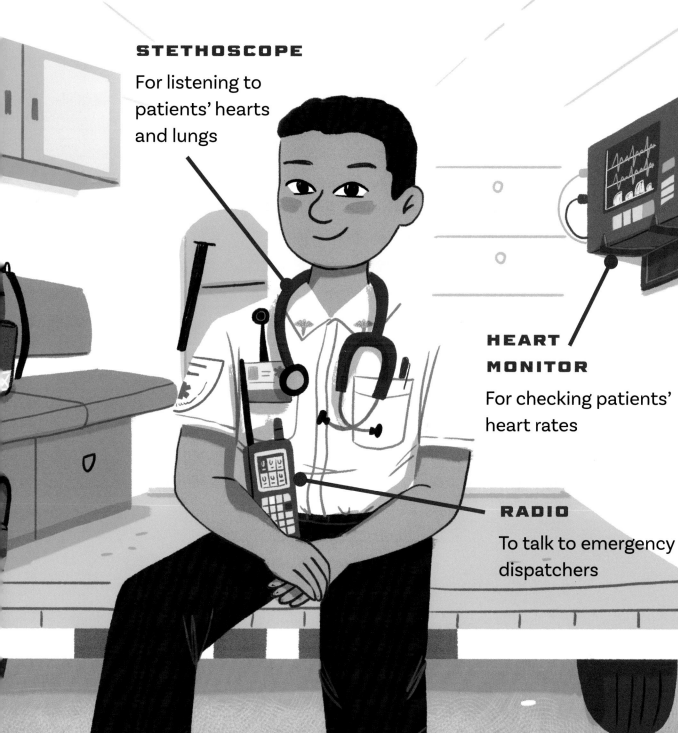

STETHOSCOPE

For listening to patients' hearts and lungs

HEART MONITOR

For checking patients' heart rates

RADIO

To talk to emergency dispatchers

I work with other healthcare and emergency workers to take care of my patients. **Meet some of the people on my team!**

CARA
PARAMEDIC
Paramedic partner

JOE AND KATE
POLICE OFFICER AND FIREFIGHTER

Firefighters and police officers often arrive at a scene before paramedics do. They provide emergency medical care before we arrive and give us information about the patient and their condition.

LEAH
EMERGENCY DISPATCHER

Gives us patients' locations and conditions

11

CHAPTER 3

A DAY AS A PARAMEDIC

I usually work a twelve-hour shift. My shift starts bright and early in the morning.

6:50 AM

I take the subway to the hospital and walk to the ambulance station. The hospital's ambulances are parked here.

AMBULANCE

I check the ambulance's supplies. Everything is fully stocked, and no medications are expired! Then Cara and I meet with the night shift paramedics. They tell us anything we need to know to start our shift.

7:00 AM

7:15 AM

Our first call comes in from Leah, the emergency dispatcher. A teenage boy was in an accident while biking. Cara and I hop in the ambulance. We're off!

7:21 AM

We get to the scene.
I check on the patient.
Cara talks to Joe to
learn what happened.
The boy's name is Noah.

"My name is Justin,"
I tell him. "I'm here to
take care of you."

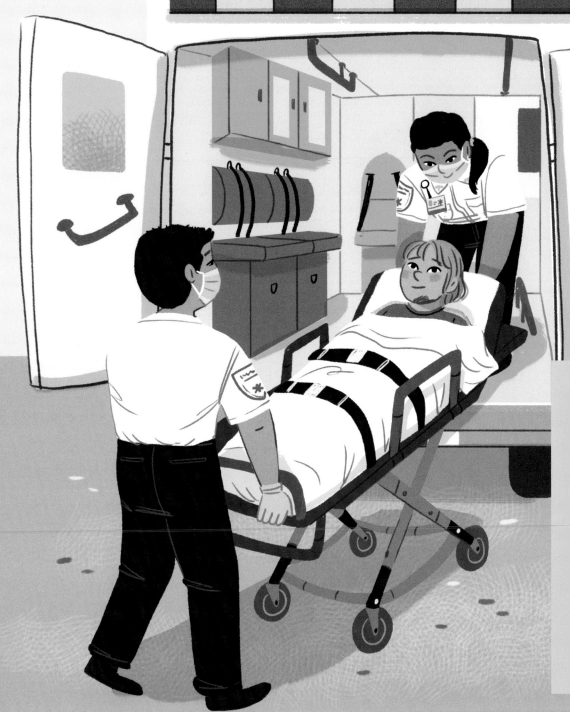

Cara and I strap Noah onto the **stretcher**. We secure the stretcher to the ambulance floor.

"The police will contact your parents," I tell Noah. "They will meet us at the hospital."

7:40 AM

Cara drives the ambulance while I care for Noah. Luckily, he isn't too badly hurt. Doctors at the hospital will make sure he doesn't have a head injury or broken bones.

7:55 AM

We bring Noah into the hospital's **ER**. We tell the doctors and nurses there what happened to Noah. We report his **vital signs** and our observations. Noah is in good hands.

10:30 AM

Our next call is for eight-month-old Iris. She has a high fever. I listen to Iris's breathing. I take her temperature. Good news! Iris doesn't need to go to the hospital. Her mother can care for her at home.

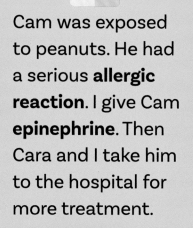

Cam was exposed to peanuts. He had a serious **allergic reaction**. I give Cam **epinephrine**. Then Cara and I take him to the hospital for more treatment.

2:30 PM

Josie had an **asthma attack** while playing soccer. I give her **oxygen** with medicine to help her breathing. Then Cara and I take her to the hospital.

21

4:00 PM

Dave is having chest pain. This can be a sign of a **heart attack**. We put Dave in the ambulance and hook him up to the heart monitor. I check his vital signs while Cara drives us to the hospital.

6:30 PM

Our shift is almost over. I put gas in the ambulance. Cara and I wash it. We restock supplies. The ambulance is ready for the next shift!

CHAPTER 4

PATIENTS COME FIRST

Another call comes in from the emergency dispatcher. The next shift's paramedics haven't arrived yet. Cara and I hop into the ambulance. If a patient needs us, our job isn't done!

Being a paramedic isn't always easy. My shifts can be long and tiring. The patients I care for are often very hurt or sick.

Still, I love my job. It's an honor when I can help someone feel better. No matter how hard my job is, I go home knowing I've helped people.

REAL-LIFE HERO!

MEET A REAL-LIFE PARAMEDIC!

NAME: Hanan Wazwaz

JOB: Paramedic

PLACE OF WORK: Mayo Clinic

What is your favorite part of being a paramedic?

I really enjoy helping my patients when they are sick and watching them feel better after I give them medicine. It's also fun when I get to work with the police and the fire department. We make a great team!

What does a paramedic do?

My first task is always making sure that my partner and I are safe. If we are not safe, then we cannot take care of our patients. Then, I do whatever I can to help my patients feel better. Sometimes, all a patient needs is for me to hold their hand. Other times, I use medications to help them feel better. It is my job to get my patients safely to a place where they can get medical care, such as a hospital. I am also responsible for making sure the hospital doctors know exactly what is going on with the patient. This makes sure the patient gets the right treatment at the hospital.

What is the hardest part about being a paramedic?

Working for twelve hours can be hard. I get tired sometimes. But I wake up right away when a patient needs my help!

What character traits do you think it's important for paramedics to have?

It's important for paramedics to always be nice to their patients and their patients' families. Paramedics must also be open-minded and willing to learn. This helps us get better at our jobs. And we should never be afraid to ask for help when we need it. Adults need help sometimes, too!

SUPERPOWER SPOTLIGHT

Health heroes have special superpowers that help them do their jobs. One of a paramedic's most important superpowers is kindness! I am patient with the people I care for and their families. I listen to them when they are talking. I do whatever I can to make my patients and their families feel better. By treating patients with kindness, I can provide them the best care possible.

HOW DO YOU SHOW KINDNESS?

GLOSSARY

allergic reaction—a response that occurs when the immune system attacks a substance that a person is allergic to. Allergic reactions can be mild or very serious.

asthma attack—the sudden swelling and narrowing of airways, making it difficult to breathe

epinephrine—a hormone that can be used as a medicine to reduce the symptoms of an allergic reaction

ER—emergency room. The ER is the department of a hospital that treats patients who need to receive care right away.

heart attack—a medical emergency that occurs when the flow of blood to the heart is blocked

oxygen—a gas in the air that humans need to live. People may be given oxygen to breathe if they are struggling to get enough of it breathing on their own.

scene—the place where something occurred

shift—a scheduled period of time that a person is at work

stretcher—a device used to move or carry a sick or injured person

vital signs—measurements of a patient's basic functions, such as heart rate, blood pressure, and temperature

LEARN MORE

Allan, John. *Let's Look at Emergency Vehicles.* Minneapolis: Hungry Tomato, 2019.

Manushkin, Fran. Super *Paramedic!* North Mankato, MN: Picture Window Books, 2019.

Moening, Kate. *EMTs.* Minneapolis: Bellwether Media, 2021.

New York City Fire Department. "Station 15 #FDNYSmart Virtual Tour for Kids." https://www.youtube.com/watch?v=hMF5nTlJOHg

PBS Learning Media. "Meet the Helpers | Paramedics Are Helpers: In-Depth." https://tpt.pbslearningmedia.org/resource/meet-the-helpers-paramedics -helpers-in-depth/meet-the-helpers-paramedics-helpers-in-depth/

INDEX